P9-DDL-478

Writing Builders

Evan and Erin Build an

ESSAY

by Amanda StJohn
illustrated by Ronnie Rooney

Content Consultant
Jan Lacina, Ph.D., College of Education
Texas Christian University

NORWOOD HOUSE PRESS
CHICAGO, ILLINOIS

Norwood House Press
P.O. Box 316598
Chicago, Illinois 60631
For information regarding Norwood House Press, please visit
our website at:
www.norwoodhousepress.com or call 866-565-2900.

Editor: Melissa York
Designer: Emily Love
Project Management: Red Line Editorial

Library of Congress Cataloging-in-Publication Data
StJohn, Amanda, 1982-
 Evan and Erin build an essay / by Amanda St. John ;
illustrated by Ronnie Rooney.
     p. cm.
 Includes bibliographical references.
 Summary: "Evan And Erin need to write an essay for school
and they share their ideas with the school librarian"--Provided
by publisher.
 ISBN-13: 978-1-59953-508-1 (library edition : alk. paper)
 ISBN-10: 1-59953-508-4 (library edition : alk. paper)
 ISBN-13: 978-1-60357-388-7 (e-book : alk. paper)
 ISBN-10: 1-60357-388-7 (e-book : alk. paper)
 1. Essay--Authorship--Juvenile literature. I. Rooney, Ronnie,
ill. II. Title.
 PN4500.S75 2012
 808.4--dc23
                        2011039360

Words in **black bold** are defined in the glossary.

Why I Like Writing Essays

I always have big ideas. Here are just a few: Kids should get to stay awake later than usual on Fridays. Aliens are scarier than most spooky monsters. It's more fun to play football outside than to play a football videogame. The world would be better if everyone had superpowers.

Writing essays is a great thing for a guy like me to know how to do. That's because essays are all about sharing big ideas with other people. My friend Erin likes to write essays with me. In an essay, by saying three reasons why our ideas are good—presto! We can convince an audience to agree with us. Wouldn't you like to do that, too?

By Evan, age 10

"Mr. Zimmer!" Evan whispered, waving the librarian over.

Evan and Erin were hard at work on their essay. Erin motioned for Mr. Zimmer to lean closer. "We just picked a **topic** for an

awesome essay. It's a secret because this idea is very good."

"Bravo! Choosing a topic is the best way to start," said Mr. Zimmer.

"We also prepared our paper with the three parts of an essay," Erin continued, "introduction, body, conclusion."

Mr. Zimmer clapped. "So, what is your big idea?"

"Well," said Evan, "Mrs. Stanley asked us to think of something that could make the world a better place. Having superpowers will make it better for sure."

"Brilliant!" Mr. Zimmer smiled. Then he rubbed his beard for a moment. "You might want to choose a few specific powers to help you prove your point."

"You're right!" exclaimed Evan. "Since we're writing a three-paragraph essay, we probably can't talk about more than two or three superpowers."

Erin knew just what to do next. "Evan, let's make a list of superpowers. We'll put a star next to the best ones."

All the Superpowers in the World
that We Can Think of:

*flying
breathing fire
move things with your
    mind
control time with a watch
change your shape into
    animals
*super strength

read people's minds
live forever
rocket boots
*heal things, even
    yourself
*laser-beam eyesight
super stretchy body

"Great list," said Mr. Zimmer. "How will you know which are the best?"

Evan and Erin whispered together before announcing a plan. "We'll make idea webs. We learned about those in class," said Evan.

"We write down our goal at the top of the paper. Then we write down the superpowers," continued Erin.

Evan added, "Last, we'll write down reasons to pick each power."

"Super," said Mr. Zimmer. "May the strongest ideas win!"

Idea Web

Goal: Choose superpowers that would make the world a better place.

FLYING
1. You can escape danger fast.
2. You can help rescue other people.
3. You won't need cars, trucks, boats, trains, or airplanes to get places.

LASER-BEAM EYESIGHT
1. You can cut things open really fast.

SUPER STRENGTH
1. You can carry anything.
2. You can hold up bridges or buildings that are about to fall down.

HEALING THINGS
1. You can save people if they are hurt, sick, or stop breathing.
2. You will never need to take medicine again.

"Hmm . . . " mused Evan. "Having laser eyesight may not be the best power ever."

"Finding out which ideas are not strong enough is what **prewriting** is all about," said Mr. Zimmer, coming back to the table. "Looks like you are ready to write a thesis statement."

"A what?" Erin looked afraid.

"Oh!" said Evan. "That's part of the introduction. It says what your big idea is."

"Now I remember," said Erin. "Like this . . ."

Introduction

Thesis:

One way to make our world a better place would be to give humans superpowers. Humans should have superpowers like flying, super strength, and healing things.

Body

"I like it!" said Evan.

"Wait a minute!" exclaimed Erin. "I used the words *humans* and *superpowers* twice."

"Let's get rid of the doubles," smiled Evan. He rewrote the thesis statement.

Thesis:
One way to make our world a better place would be to give humans superpowers like flying, super strength, and healing things.

"Great **revision**," said Mr. Zimmer. "Time to write a first draft of the body!"

"We can start our outline with what we wrote in the idea web," agreed Evan.

Erin started writing. When she was finished, she set down her pencil.

OUTLINE

Thesis: One way to make our world a better place would be to give humans superpowers like flying, super strength, and healing things.

Superpower 1: Flying
A. You can escape danger fast.
B. You can help rescue other people.
C. You won't need cars, trucks, boats, trains, or airplanes to get places.

Superpower 2: Super strength
A. You can carry anything.
B. You can hold up bridges or buildings that are about to fall down.

Superpower 3: Healing things
A. You can save people if they are hurt, sick, or stop breathing.
B. You will never need to take medicine again.

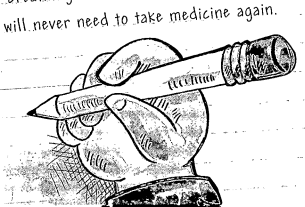

"I really like our new outline!" exclaimed Erin. "Now we just have to rewrite these points into complete sentences for our essay!"

Evan picked up the pencil and waved it around. "My turn!"

Evan rewrote the information from the outline in his notebook in the section labeled "Body."

He started adding, erasing, and crossing out words. "I'll make complete sentences and cross out the parts that repeat ideas."

BODY:

Having these superpowers would be a great gift. If a bridge started to fall into a river, flying people could escape fast. They could rescue other people, too. We could heal a hurt person instantly. Can you guess what else would happen if people had these three special powers? We wouldn't need cars, trucks, boats, trains, or airplanes anymore. Everyone would fly everywhere. We could carry everything. We would never have to take cough syrup because we could just heal the cough ourselves.

Mr. Zimmer smoothed his beard and read the paragraph. "Looking good. How about writing the rest of the introduction next? The first line of an essay should be the **hook**. The hook grabs the reader's attention. Then they'll want to read the whole paper."

"So we could start the essay with a joke," offered Erin.

"Yes," said Mr. Zimmer. "That's called humor."

The two kids tapped their pencils, thinking.

Erin looked up. "Hey, Evan! Don't you wish you could have superpowers?"

"I wish that all the time," Evan answered with wide eyes.

"Great! I think I just found a hook for this essay."

Evan and Erin put their thesis together with the rest of their introduction. Then Erin began the conclusion. "Do we need a hook here, Evan?"

"No," he shook his head. "First we'll say our thesis again, but in a new way, so readers remember what we were talking about."

"How about, 'Flying, super strength, and healing things are the ultimate powers'?"

"Good one!" replied Evan. "Now, we need to leave our readers with one more idea so that they will keep thinking about our topic."

Evan and Erin high-fived. The draft was ready to be copied onto clean notebook paper. "Let's call it . . . *Superpowers Can Change the World*," suggested Erin.

Evan quickly wrote the title at the top of the paper.

Superpowers Can Change the World!

Don't you wish you could have superpowers? My friend and I want them for sure. We know that some superheroes, like Spiderman, were born without special powers. Then, one day—presto! The superhero gets magical powers and uses them to make a neighborhood safer. One way to make our world a better place would be to give humans superpowers like flying, super strength, and healing things.

Having these superpowers would be a great gift. If a bridge started to fall into a river, flying people could escape fast. If they had super strength, they could rescue other people, too. Suppose a flying kid rescued someone from the river, but he or she stopped breathing. How could a kid save her life? Well, if the kid could heal things, then she would just heal the person instantly. Can you guess what else would happen if people had these three powers?

We wouldn't need cars or trucks anymore. Everyone would fly to the grocery store. Even a baby could carry groceries because it would be super strong. We would never buy cough syrup again because we could just heal the cough ourselves.

Flying, having super strength, and healing things are the ultimate powers. They could help people live better in all different ways. But here's one more thought: if we can heal people, we can heal animals and plants, too. Just imagine how beautiful our world would become if everyone was given superpowers.

"There's only one thing left to do," Evan said.

"Share our secret essay with everyone!" clapped Erin.

You Can Build an Essay, Too!

STEP 1: The Big Idea. Choose a topic to write about. What big ideas would you like to explore?

STEP 2: Prewriting. Make lists to explore your ideas. Create webs to add to your ideas and organize them.

STEP 3: First Draft. There are three parts to an essay. Each one has a job to do. Fold a piece of paper into three parts. Label the sections introduction, body, and conclusion. Using your lists and webs, begin developing paragraphs.

The **Introduction** tells what you are *about to say* in your essay. It has a hook that makes your audience want to read more. It reveals your big idea.

The **Body** tells what you *are saying*. It has a main sentence. It explains your big idea more clearly or proves your big idea is a good one.

The **Conclusion** tells *what you just said* in the body. It repeats the big idea, but in a new way. It gives the audience something to think about.

STEP 4: Revise. Look over your draft. Does it make sense? Can you cut out some words? Do you need to add some more information? Does each paragraph have a main sentence and supporting details? Share your draft with a friend. Ask them to share one question they still have about your draft.

STEP 5: Final Draft. Once you feel your draft is complete, neatly copy it onto notebook paper or type it into a computer. Be sure to share your big idea with others.

Try a five-paragraph essay if you'd like a greater challenge. As a five-paragraph essay, Evan and Erin's superpower paper would be organized like this:

Paragraph 1: One way to make our world a better place would be to give humans superpowers such as the ability to fly, be super strong, and heal things.

Paragraph 2: All about flying.

Paragraph 3: All about incredible strength.

Paragraph 4: All about healing things.

Paragraph 5: Flying, having super strength, and healing things are the ultimate powers.

Glossary

hook: a fact, quote, question, or joke that captures a reader's attention.

prewriting: part of the writing process that explores your thoughts about a topic.

revision: a change that strengthens what you've written.

topic: the big idea.

For More Information

Books

Olien, Rebecca. *Kids Write!: Fantasy & Sci Fi, Mystery, Autobiography, Adventure & More! (Williamson Kids Can! Series)*. Nashville, TN: Williamson Publishers, 2005.

TIME For Kids: Ready, Set, Write! New York: TIME for Kids, 2006.

Websites

2011 Hands-On Explorer Challenge Winning Essay Excerpts
http://kids.nationalgeographic.com/kids/stories/
peopleplaces/hands-on-explorer-challenge-2011-winning-
essay-excerpts/
National Geographic Kids has an annual essay contest—
check out the 2011 winners here.

Outline of the Five-Paragraph Essay
http://www.gc.maricopa.edu/English/essay/
This online outline explains the parts of a five-paragraph essay.

About the Author

Amanda StJohn is a writer living in Saint Paul, Minnesota. She dreams of flying over the state's 10,000 lakes and landing on top of the moon.